SHUKR ITS REALITY

AURANG ZEB AZMI

KITAB BHAVAN
NEW DELHI-110002

Kitab Bhavan
Publishers, Distributors, Exporters & Importers
1784, Kalan Mahal, Darya Ganj
New Delhi-110002 (India)

Phone : (91-11) 3277392/93, 3274686
Web Site: www.kitabbhavan.com
E-mail : nasri@vsnl.com
Fax : (91-11) 3263383

First Edition : 2004

ISBN : 81-7151-352-2

Laser Typesetting at:
Ad Concept
822, Katra Hiddu, Farash Khana,
Delhi-110006

Published in India by:
Nusrat Ali Nasri for Kitab Bhavan
1784, Kalan Mahal, Darya Ganj
New Delhi-110002 [India]

Printed in India at:
Nice Printing Press
Khureji Khas, Delhi-110051

To ,

My sister

Fãṭimah Al-Zarrín

To whom the credit of my higher education goes. May Allah prolong her life and give me time to serve her.

A. Z. Azmi

CONTENTS

ABBREVIATIONS

AD	:	Abu Daud
AR	:	Alaihir Rahmah
B	:	Bukhari
DH	:	Al Dhahbi
JS	:	Al Jami Al Saghir
M	:	Muslim
MZ	:	Majma Al Zawaid
N	:	Nasai
RS	:	Riyad al-Salihin
RA	:	Raziallahu Anhu
SAWS	:	Sallalahu Alaihi Wa Sallam
T	:	Tirmidhi
TR	:	Targhib

PREFACE

What's man? He is an advanced shape of a sperm-drop. A sperm-drop that first became a lump of flesh then there were added to it the bones and this became to be called " the new born child ". All these stages along with other qualities happened in the womb of the mother by the help of the Only God Allah, the Almighty. It is His boon that he was granted the love of his parents, especially, the mother.

After all this, He granted him the wisdom and the power to differentiate the good from the bad and the useful from the useless. Being experienced through the parents and the kind teachers, he became able to study his surroundings and then to take lessons from it.

What are these surroundings of the world and these universes? Who created these and why? We know that these universes are created in six periods of time and we also know that these are only for this living creature; man. He has been permitted to use and utilize these as he wishes. These are under his control and at his service.

This kind of service and voluntary co-operation is a clear evidence that there is a Power that has brought all these. It is He Who has ordered to cooperate with the desire of this collection of flesh, bones, mind and free will. As if these are speaking out by their activities that there is

Some One Whom they adore.

Now, the question that arises is that when all these things are functioning as per the order of their Creator and Lord then why does not this man do things according to His will. One would infer this if he studies carefully the signs Allah has created in man and the others. Truthfully, He said: " I did not create the jinn and the mankind but to worship Me "

Apart from these evidences, there are living examples of the pious people whose reality, ability, truthfulness and piousness are recognized by the wise inhabitants of this world.

The All Merciful God did not only bestow these but He indicated by these urging him to select the right way and to worship Him. It was done through the books revealed to His Messengers and Prophets.

After all these, He did not let go His servants free from restrictions but put them to tests that they shall necessarily have to pass before achieving the ultimate goal i.e Jannah.

Now, there is left nothing. A man can choose the way he prefers and desires. If he gives thanks then it will return to himself and if he denies his God then it is his own fault: "That those who died might die after a clear sign and that those who lived might live after a clear sign"

Being full of this sentiment of gratitude, I have tried to discuss, as I could, this matter in the light of the Holy Qur'an and the Traditions of the Prophet (SAWS). I hope that the readers will also take it similarly. We all pray that which was taught Muaz by the Prophet (SAWS):

" O Allah! Help me on Your remembrance, thanks and good worship"

May Allah grant us wisdom to give thanks to Him and to His servants as well.

A. Z. Azmi

The Meaning and Significance

Islam has influenced the Arabic language greatly and in different ways. It changed its styles and contents. It played a great role in the development of its real speakers. This is a topic in itself that requires volumes. Even its one side of styles is so wide that would not be covered in a book. At present, I want to talk about its influence on the Arabic words. Apart from giving several words, it changed the meaning of some words or it gave another meaning that is altogether different from the previous one but has a deep relation to it. For instance, Salah, Seyam and Zakah. The word "Salah" was used, in the classical Arabic, for being close to the fire[1] but Islam gave it another good meaning and used it for being close to Allah in a proper way that is taught by the Prophet. "Seyam" was used for abandoning the animals especially camels and horses, for some days in lonely places, to train them[2]. So that if they were in a place where there is no food and water they could live and work. The atmosphere and environment of the Arabian deserts is like that. "Zakah" is a word that means, in the classical Arabic language, to grow and to be pure. When Islam came it ordained it to give part of money or some other thing from the whole to make it pure and grow in the Islamic way. "Shukr" is also like that. In the beginning, it meant to feed an animal with some small quantity and expect to get a big quantity of milk[3] but when

Islam came it used it in another "new" meaning and that is a sentiment that arises from taking lesson, from the miracles of the bodies, sights of the creatures and occurrences of the history.

It is the opposite of "Kufr" (Paganism) because it is paganism, which distances men from all these qualities. The Prophet Mohammad said:

" He who does not thank people does not thank Allah" [4]

We also came across in the chapter of 'Al Muminun':

" It is He who has created for you the ears, eyes, and hearts; little thanks it is ye give" [5]

So "Shukr" is all light and belief while "Kufr" is all darkness and apostasy. An Arabic poet has said: Tolerance is good only in its places and liberality is good (suit) only that who thanks."

---

1) Even the Qur'an also used it in this meaning. See 84:13, 87:13, 111:3, 17:18, 4:10, 14:29, 38:56, 58:8, 82:15

2) Several poets used it in this meaning. See Tafsir *Tadabbur-e-Qur'an 1/445*

3) Lisan al Arab " ShKR"

4) T, 1954

5) '78

Difference between "Hamd" and "Shukr"

Some scholars have differentiated between "Hamd" and "Shukr". They say that "Hamd" is limited and is especial to God but "Shukr" is common to all. They also say that "Shukr" comes as a result of some good done to the "Shakir" (Thanks-giver) whereas "Hamd" is not like that. It is necessary whether some one is bestowed with blessings or not.[1] But , to me, these two words come as a consequence of any good done to the thank- giver[2]. Ibn Abbas has said:

"Hamd" is nothing but "Shukr"[3]

The evidences of "Shukr" will be given in this booklet but as for the evidences of "Hamd", these are as follows:

1-It has been mentioned in the first chapter:

"Praise be to Allah, the Cherisher, and Sustainer of the Worlds: Most Gracious, Most Merciful" [4].

Here the word "Hamd" is mentioned after these actions.

2-Our Prophet Mohammad has taught us the prayer after taking food:

"Praise be to Allah Who gave us to eat, drink, and made us of the Muslims" [5].

3-In another tradition, we read that when some one's son is dead and he takes patience and thanks God then

God orders His angels to build a 'House of thanks' (Baitul-Hamd) in the Jannah.[6]

These three evidences are a strong proof that this word has a meaning similar to that of "Shukr".

---

1) Idahul Qur'an 92-95
2) It is also clear from the coming tradition in which the word "Hamd" is used for men: " Abdullah s/o Abu Rabiah (RA) narrates that the Prophet (SAWS) took a loan of forty thousand from me. Then when the money came to him he paid it back to me saying: May Allah bless you in your family and money. The return of the loan is nothing but to praise and to pay" N, 4687
3) Maulana Asharaf Ali Thanvi: Mukammal Bayanul Qur'an Vol. I, P I. In this chapter refferd to, the author has proved the same view as of mine. (Azmi)
4) 1 :2-4
5) A, AD,T
6) T, 1021

The importance of Shukr and its priority

Shukr has a great importance in Islam. It is the foundation stone of the religion, Islam. It is the base of monotheism and the faith. Our Lord 'Allah' says:

" Praise be to Allah' to Whom belong all things in the heavens and on earth: to Him be praise in the Hereafter; and he is All-Wise, All-Aware"[1]

He further says:

" What can Allah gain by your punishment? If ye are grateful and ye believe? Nay, it is Allah that recogniseth (all good), and knoweth all things"[2].

The first verse speaks that the man accepted the oneness of God only when a sentiment of Shukr inundated his heart.

As for "If ye are grateful and ye believe" of the second verse, it makes abundantly clear that Shukr begets faith.

All that I have said is also clear from the arrangement and coherence of the Qur'anic verses. Recite Al-Fatiha, the first chapter of the Holy Qur'an, where He has said:

"Praise be to Allah the Cherisher and Sustainer of the Worlds: Most Gracious Most Merciful; Master of the Day of Judgment Thee do we worship, and Thine aid we seek. Show us the straight way, the way of those on whom Thou hath bestowed Thy Grace, those whose (portion) is not wrath. And who go not astray"[3].

Then the first thing mentioned here is thanks-giving. So it is the base of monotheism and the base of belief in the prophethood because the real and proper guidance is not possible except by the Prophet.

Then it is the base of worship and good deed as well as it is the base of religion and monotheism. Allah says:

" O ye who believe! Eat of the good things that We have provided for you. And be grateful to Allah, it is Him ye worship."[4]

Allah says in another place:

" -----Then seek ye sustenance from Allah, serve Him, and be grateful to him: to Him will be your return."[5]

In another place, He says considering it the base of good deed:

"So he smiled, amused at her speech; and he said: " O my Lord! So order me that I may be grateful for Thy favours, which Thou have bestowed on me and on my parents, and that I may work the righteousness that will pleas Thee: and admit me, by Thy Grace, to the ranks of Thy righteous Servants"[6]

And Salah is also a kind of remembrance. He says:

" ---And establish regular prayer for My remembrance."[7]

And becoming of remembrance as Shukr is very clear from the order of this verse:

"Then do ye remember Me; I will remember you. Be grateful to Me, and reject not Faith"[8]

---

1) 34:1
2) 4: 147
3) 1:2-7
4) 2:172
5) 29:17
6) 27:19
7) 20:14
8) 2:152

For Allah Only

Before discussing any other thing, let us make clear that only doing any good thing towards man, beast or God cannot result any good thing. To achieve any good or eternal goal requires that the aim should be very clear. I mean that it would be directed towards Allah, whatever the matter is. If you do any good job but you do not realize Allah during that it would not be beneficial especially in the coming life i.e. the Hereafter. And if you do any good and reasonable thing, although it seams bad, it would result in good in this world and in the coming also. I mention below a tradition that speaks of what I said earlier:

"Abu Ishaq Zuhri (RA) said: The Messenger of Allah (SAWS) came to me to look after me in the year of "Hijjatul-Wida"'. I was suffering from a severe pain. I said: 0 the Messenger of Allah: You see what a severe pain has struck me. I am also a rich man. I have no heir except this daughter of mine. Can I give two third of my money as alms. He replied: No, I said: Then half, 0 the Messenger of Allah. He replied in negative. I said: Then one third, 0 the Messenger of Allah. He replied: yes it is too much. That you may leave your heirs rich is Better than that you may leave them poor begging before the other persons. Every thing, which you spend for the sake of Allah, would give you good reward even that you put into the mouth of your wife. He narrated that he said: O the Messenger of Allah: can I make any one of my friends as caretaker. He replied: Every thing that you leave for the sake of Allah would lift you a step------"[1]

Go through this tradition deeply. It tells you aloud that that word, either personal or common or religion, done for the sake of Allah sincerely goes directly to God and its reward is perfect. In the above-mentioned tradition, the doer is limited within the boundaries of his family. As for the religious and common affairs, there are a number of Qur'anic verses and prophetic sayings that point out this fact. Read the traditions regarding sacred war (Jihad) and verses related to the worship of God.

---

1) R, 7

Shukr As The Best Thing In Both The Worlds

It has been proved by the aforesaid that thanks to Allah is the first and the foremost duty of a humanbeing, and that it has covered all kinds of mundane and divine things. It means that thanks is the only thing in this world and in the Hereafter and hence thanks is the best thing in both the worlds. Keeping this in view, the Prophet Mohammad (SAWS) regarded a heart full of gratitude as one of the best four things in both the worlds. He said:

"There are four things, if these have been given to anyone then as though he has been given the best thing of the world and the Hereafter. These are a thankful heart, remembering tongue, patient body at the time of the examination and a wife that cheats neither about herself nor regarding his (her husband's) money"[1]

It is further strengthened by the fact that the Qur'an begins with 'Al-Fatihah' which is nothing but thanks-giving and finishes with 'Al-Ikhlas' which is also an expression of thanks-giving. This adequately clarifies that the Book of Allah and the constitution of this mundane life and which comprises guidelines for this and the Hereafter, bracketed with verses reminding us to pay your gratitude to Him.

If you think upon this order deeply you will find another clear fact. That is that the thanks is core and essence of all worships and religious deeds. It is the centre around which all religious and worldy matters move and if anyone miss this one or avoides it he may miss the main and basic thing.

---

1) TB, 4/502

Be Thankful

In view of all these benefits and advantages flowing from thanks who would not like to be thankful? None of us would like to be ingrate. The Prohhet replied when he was asked about his incessant worship and prayers:

"Should I not be a thankful servant ---."[1]

But here is a question that if someone has nothing to pay the duty of the thanks to anyone then what would he do? It has also been answered by the Prophet himself as follows:

-That you should praise that doer:

"The Messenger of Allah said: "He who has been given any favour, he should do the same if he can and if he cannot then he should praise him because he who praises, discharges his duty of gratitude and he who hides it, commits ingratitude." [2]

-That you should pray Allah for him:

"The Messenger of Allah said: "He who asks Allah's protection, he should be given that and he who asks by the name of Allah he should be given, he who calls you for help he should be answered and he who did any good thing to you, you should repay him similarly and if you cannot pray Allah for him".[3]

Here lies another fact on which the whole religious

philosophy is based. That is rights of God and His servants. There are only two kinds of rights in Islam mainly rights of God and rights of the people. Rights of God are to worship Him in time and rights of the people are to help them and to consider them at any corner.

And it is fact that the rights of God are incomplete untill you pay the rights of the people. That's why Islam lays stress upon Salah and Zakah at a time. Salah is the right of God while Zakah is the right of the people.

---

1) R, 61
2) AD, 4813
3) R, 652-653

Call For Beneficence

In view of the importance of Shukr, Allah and His Prophet, Mohammad (SAWS) have urged us, the humanbeing, to do good to every apparition of life. Severely man has been urged to do good. It has been abundantly made clear that even 'intention' of doing good is rewarded. The Prophet has said:

" He who intended to do good but did not, Allah would register a good reward for him and if he intended and did, He would note ten good rewards up to seven hundred times up to numberless times-."[1]

The Prophet has tought that real Islam would always urge a true Muslim to do only good to others. He said:

"Abdullah s/o Amr s/o Al-'As narrates that a man asked the Messenger of Allah: Which kind of Islam is the best? He replied: It is to feed (someone) and to greet whom you knew and whom you did not recognize."[2]

Here are some kinds of beneficence and kindness:

1-To help the poor:

" The Messenger of Allah said: "The Muslim is the brother of the Muslim. He neither wrongs him nor does he surrender him (to the enemy). He who helps his brother is helped by Allah -----."[3]

2- To look after the orphan or the widow:

" The Prophet said: " The person who works hard for

the widow or the poor is like the one who fights in the way of Allah"[4]

3-To pray to avoid war:

" -- 0 the people! Do not desire to face the enemies and pray for safety but if you fight, be patient and note that the paradise lies in the shades of the swords.[5]

4-To do good even to the beasts and birds:

" The Messenger of Allah said: " A man felt thirsty while he was going somewhere. He found a well and came down to it and drank. When he came out he saw a dog lolling his tongue and eating dewdrops. He thought that this dog is suffering from such thirst as that of mine. He went down the well, filled his shoes with water and poured it into his mouth. The dog thanked Allah for this and he was pardoned."[6]

" The Messenger of Allah stopped the people from imprisoning the animals to death."[7]

As a rule for the people he summed up saying" Every good thing is alms".[8]

---

1) R, 8-9
2) M,21
3) R, 122
4) R, 137-138
5) R, 3'1
6) R, 72
7) R, 613
8) R, 70-1

EVIDENCES OF SHUKR

Boons and favours of Allah are innumerable. These are beyond imagination and human thought. Pointing out these facts, Allah says thus:

"----but if ye count the favours of Allah, never will ye be able to enumerate them. Verily, man is given up to injustice and ingratitude"[1]

It is more clear and elaborated in the chapter titled "Luqman":

" And if all the trees on earth were pens and the ocean (were ink), with seven oceans behind it to add to its (supply), yet would not the Words of Allah be exhausted (in the writing) : for Allah is Exalted in Power, Full of Wisdom"[2]

It becomes clear from these verses that the boons and favours of Allah and His blessings are numberless. None of us can count them neither in learning nor remembrance nor in writing.

These boons are not only beyond counting but also of different kinds and hues. On this basis, He provokes us to take lesson from that and to pay thanks to Him. He says:

" O Children of Israel! Call to mind the (special) favour which I bestowed upon you, and fulfill your Covenant"[3]

In the chapter "Al Doha" He addresses His Prophet telling him to thank Him:

" But the Bounty of thy Lord --Rehearse and proclaim"[4]

When we look upon these verses we find that the Almighty Allah did not exhort to thank only after He mentioned these boons and gifts of His. These boons are like evidences on giving thank to him who has extended them to the humanbeings.

Now I want to count some of thanks-related evidences in a categorized way so that the measuring of Shukr should be easier and clearer also.

---

1) 14:34
2) 31:27
3) 2:40
4) 93:11

Evidences from the Universe

God has created the whole of universe; stars, oceans, plants, skies and animals etc. Then He put it at the disposal of the mankind to make use of these and to thank Him for His favours. He says pointing out the food stuffs provided to him:

"O ye who believe! Eat of the good things that We have provided for you, and be grateful to Allah, if Him ye worship"[1]

He further says indicating to the means of comfort and convenience:

"And it is He Who made the night and the day to follow each other: for such as desire to be mindful or to show their gratitude"[2]

In another place He says:

"It is out of His mercy that He has made for you night and day, that ye may rest therein, and that ye may seek of His grace and in order that ye may be grateful"[3]

In the chapter 'Al-Rum' He says:

"Among His singns is this, that He sends the winds, and heralds of glad tidings, giving you a taste of his mercy,-that the ships may sail by His command

and that ye may seek of His bounty: in order that ye may be grateful"[4]

In the Chapter 'Yasin' He has said shown the life of the earth which dies due to lack of water:

"A sign for them is the earth that is dead: We do give it life, and produce grain thereform, of which ye do eat. And we produce therein orchards with datepalms and vines, and we cause springs to gush forth therein; that they may enjoy the fruits of this (artistry): it was not their hands that made this: will they not then give thanks? [5]

In another place of this chapter, He says:

" See they not that it is We Who have created for them-among the things which Our hands have fashioned-cattle, which are under their dominion- And that We have subjected them to their (use)? Of them some do carry them and some they eat: and they have (other) profits from them (besides), and they get (milk) to drink, will they not then be grateful" [6]

In the chapter of "Ghafir", He says:

" It is Allah Who has made the night for you, that ye may rest therein, and the day, to give you light. Verily, Allah is full of grace and bounty to man: yet most men give no thanks"[7]

In the chapter of 'Al-Rahman', you see that He counts for man each and every boon of His and then throws the gauntlet to deny them or any of them. He says:

" The Most Gracious! It is He Who has taught the Qur'an. He has created man: He has taught him intelligent speech. The sun and the moon follow courses (exactly) computed; and the herbs and the trees- both (alike) bow in adoration. And the Firmament has He raised high, and He has set up the (Balance) of justice, in order that ye may not transgress (due) balance. So establish weight with justice and fall not short in the balance. It is He Who has spread out the earth for His creatures: Therein is fruit and date-palms, producing spatches (enclosing dates); also corn, with (its) leaves and stalk for fodder, and sweet-smelling plants" [8]

After all these boons and favours provided for human being, He says:

" Then which of the favours of thy Lord will ye deny?

This verse has been repeated after mentioning every gift given to the mankind as if He is indicating to every boon by finger and asking man who denies His worship: Which kind of boons will you deny? [9]

It is the last way of sympathy caused by anyone. God who is full of sympathy and grace extends the hands of mercy and takes the man in a way, full of grace, guiding him towards that which is right and resulting in the "great success"[10] i.e. the Jannah. If anyone does not apply with right rules and follows the zigzag way he would be considered as oppressor and wrong-doer by every man that enjoys with the wisdom.

---

1) 2:172
2) 25:62
3) 28:73
4) 30:46
5) 36:33-35
6) 36:71-73
7) 40:61
8) 55:1-12
9) 55:13
10) 4:13, 9:89, 100, 61:12 etc.

EVIDENCES FROM THE HUMAN BODY

It is a very famous saying that "He who recognizes himself recognizes his Lord". It means that a person who thinks about himself and who studies himself and his body, he would find it easy to recognize God.

That's why we see that the Almighty Allah exhorts man to think about himself, to recall the different stages of his life and then to take lesson from within himself. All these things are not but only to know Lord, to worship Him and to praise Him for that. He says:

" And remember, We delivered you from the people of Pharaoh: they set you hard task and chastisement, slaughtered your sons and let your womenfolk live; therein was a tremendous trial from your Lord. And remember We divided the sea for you and saved you and drowned Pharaoh's people within your very sight. And remember We appointed forty mights for Moses, and in his absence ye took the calf (for worship), and ye did grievous wrong. Even then We did forgive you, there was a chance for you to be grateful"[1]

He added saying:

" And remember ye said: " O Moses! We shall never believe in thee until we see Allah manifestly "

Thereupon thunderbolt seized you. Then We raised you up after your death; ye had the chance to be grateful" [2]

He also said:

" It is He Who brought you forth from the wombs of your mothers when ye knew nothing; and He gave you hearing and sight and intelligence and affections: that ye may give thanks to (Allah) [3].

In the chapter of 'Al-Mominun', He says:

" It is he Who has created for you (the faculties of) hearing, sight, feeling and understanding; little thanks it is ye give" [4]

In the chapter of "Al-Insan", He says:

" Has there not been over man a long period of time, when he was nothing- (not even) mentioned? Verily We created man from a drop of mingled sperm, in order to try him: so We gave him the (gifts), of hearing and sight. We showed him the Way: whether he be grateful or ungrateful"[5]

In 'Al-Zumr', He says:

He created you (All) from a single person: then created, of like nature, his mate; and He sent down for you eight heads of cattle in pairs: He created you , in the wombs of your mothers, in stages , one after another, in three veils of darkness. Such is Allah, your Lord and Cherisher: to Him belongs (All) dominion. There is no god but He: then how are ye turned away (from your true Lord)? If ye reject (Allah), truly Allah hath no need of you; but He liketh not ingratitude from His servants: if ye are grateful He is pleased with you. No bearer of burdens can bear of burden of another. [6]

There are a lot of proofs in the Holy Qur'an , which say clearly that the body of man is a great evidence to prove that the Almighty Allah is present and He is worth worship.

That's why he has to pay for every part of it in this short-termed world. The Prophet (SAWS) said:

" A man has three hundred and sixty joints. He has to give free-will offering for every part of his. They asked: Who can do it? He replied: That's to bury the spit in the mosque and to remove the hindrance from the way and if you do not find it then the two Rak'ats (Two bows) will be enough for it "[7]

And a man will be asked about the use of himself on the Day of Resurrection:

" The Messenger of Allah said: The feet of a servant do not leave its place on the Day of Resurrection until he would be asked about his life where he spent, his knowledge what he did of it, his money from where he earned it and where he spent it and his body where he used it?" [8]

On this basis the Qur'an names those who do not pay any attention to God and to the good deeds as those who transgress themselves. It is because that their bodies and other parts of their bodies indicate to the eixistence of a Creater worth worship only. Avoidance of this indication is denial of the order of worship, passed by the human body itself.

---

1) 2:49-52
2) 2:55-56
3) 16:78
4) 23:78
5) 76:1-3
6) 39:6-7
7) AD, 5242
8) T, 241

EVIDENCES FROM THE HISTORY

The Almighty Allah has given a number of news of prophets and great personalities who thanked Him and left good and adoptable footprints in this field. It came about Ibrahim (AS):

" Abraham was indeed a model, devoutly obedient to Allah, (And) true in faith, and he joined not gods with Allah. He showed his gratitude for the favours of Allah." [1]

In the same chapter, He said:

" Then We revealed to thee " follow the ways of Abraham the True in faith, and he joined not gods with Allah" [2]

About Nuh, He said:

" O ye that are sprung from those whom we carried in the (Ark) with Noah! Verily he was a devotee, most grateful"[3]

Daud and Sulaiman (AS) were also mentioned in this list:

" We gave knowledge to David and Solomon: and they both said: " Praise be to Allah, Who has favoured us above many of His servants who believe" [4]

He added to that saying:

" Said one who had knowledge of the Book: "I will bring

it to thee before ever thy glance retuns to thee." Then when (Solomon) saw it placed firmly before him, he said: " This is by the grace of my Lord!to test me whether I am grateful or ungrateful! And if any is grateful, truly his gratitude is (a gaiy for his own soul; but if any is ungrateful, truly my Lord is free of all needs, supreme in Honour" [5]

The Prophet Mohammad, who is a recognized prophet by all religious scholars, was also a beautiful symbol for that. He advised all humanbeings, Arabs and non-Arabs, to heed towards which is good and reasonable and to avoid that is bad and baseless. He himself said: "Take what is pure and leave what is impure. The Almighty Allah says about his being a symbol of thanks and praise and for those who want Him and the life-after:

" Ye have indeed in the Messenger of Allari an excellent example for him who hopes in Allah and the Final Day, and who remembers Allah much" [6]

---

1) 16:120-121
2) 16:123
3) 17:3
4) 27:15
5) 27:40
6) 33:21

Evidences from the Guidance

When a sentiment of praise for God arises in the heart and mind of a humanbeing, he searches for a proper way that can guide him towards his aim and can please the One Who has created him and thus can ensure a life that is eternal, and ever lasting. The Creator watches all these actions of His creature. He becomes sympathetic to him and guides him directly or indirectly to the path that leads to His pleasure. The prophet Yusuf has pointed out that reality saying:

" And I follow the ways of my fathers,-Abraham, Isaac, and Jacob; and never could we attribute any partners whatever to Allah: that (comes) of the grace of Allah to us and to mankind: yet most men are not grateful"

On this direct way of guidance, He urges man to thank Him:

"And hold fast, all together, by the rope which Allah (stretches out for you), and be not divided among yourselves; and remember with gratitude Allah's favour on you; for ye were enemies and he joined your hearts in love, so that, by His grace, ye became brethren; and ye were on the brink of the pit of Fire, and he saved you from it. Thus doth Allah make His signs clear to you: that ye may be guided" [2]

As for the indirect way of guidance i.e. by prophecy and message, the prophet Musa says urging his native people to praise and thank Him:

" Remember Moses said to his people: " O my people! Call in remembrance the favour of Allah unto you, when He produced prophets among you, made you kings, and gave you what He had not given to any other among the peoples" [3]

There is another way of guidance or an advanced way of that and that is revealing of scriptures upon those who are selected for that. It is a more everlasting method than that of the prophecy. The Almighty Allah points out this fact saying thus:

" Praise be to Allah, Who has sent to His servant the Book, and hath allowed therein no Crookedness: (He hath made it) straight (And clear) in order that He may warn (the godless) of a terrible punishment from Him, and that He may give glad tidings to the believers who work righteous deeds, that shall have a goodly reward" [4]

Then we should praise and thank Allah who gave us guidance directly by inspiration or indirectly by His messengers and scriptures that were revealed [5] to them.

---

1) 12:38
2) 3:103
3) 5:20
4) 18:1-2
5) That's why the Prophet said that the study of the Holy Qur'an does not mean to know that is contained in it but to work accordingly:
"Many those who understand the religion but they are not those who understand it really and the person whom his knowledge did not benefit his ignorance harmed him. Read the Holy Qur'an till he prohibits you (from the sin) and if he does not prohibit you, you are not really reader of it" MZ, 1/440

THANKS OF THE OTHER CREATURES

Before proceeding to any other topic, we have to note a great proof on this matter and that is the thanks of other creatures of God. You see these universes, air, angel, water, plants, and animals. All these creatures are working in their natural way. The air is blowing, the water is flowing, the plants are growing and the birds are singing. Do you understand all this? These are the ways of their worship. They are doing their prayer as they have been ordained. Then blowing of air is by the command of God and falling of the rain is by His command. It means that all these creatures are busy in carrying out what they have been ordered although we do not know their modes of prayer. The Almighty Allah indicates to this fact:

" Each one knows its own (mode of) prayer and praise. And Allah knows well all that they do"[1]

In another place He has said:

" The seven heavens and the earth, and all beings therein, declare His glory. There is not a thing but celebrates His praise; and yet ye understand not how they declare His glory" [2]

It means that all creatures of God pray to Him. None of these can move a bit against the will of God, He says:

"Whatever beings there are in the heavens and on the earth do prostrate themselves to Allah-with good-will" [3]

In the chapter of 'Al-Nur' He says:

" Seest thou not that it is Allah Whose praises all

beings in the heavens and on the earth do celebrate, and the birds (of the air) with wings outspread" [4]

In the chapter of 'Al-Rum' He has said:

"To Him belongs every being that is in the heavens and on the earth: all are devoutly obedient to Him" [5]

Further in 'Al-Rahman' He says:

" The sun and the moon follow courses (exactly) computed" [6]

In 'Al-Zumar' the prayer of angel has been mentioned:

"And thou wilt see the angels surrounding the Throne (Divine) on all sides, singing glory and praise to their Lord. The decision between them (At Judgment) will be in (perfect) justice, and the cry (on all sides) will be, " Praise be to Allah, the Lord of the worlds"[7]

In 'Al-Ra'd', the praise of lightning and thunderbolt is quoted:

" Nay, thunder repeateth His praises, and so do the angels, with awe: He flingeth the loudvoiced thunder-bolts, and therewith He striketh whomsoever He will...yet these (are the men) the while they are disputing about Allah He is Mighty in Power" [8]

So all of these thank their Creator in their way, which is unknown to us. This is a great evidence for these who do not thank God.

---

1) 24:41
2) 17:44
3) 13:15
4) 24:41
5) 30:26
6) 55:5
7) 39:75
8) 13:13

AMAZEMENT AT THE INFIDELITY

If a person fails to thank Allah despite all that underlined in the foregoing and he does not praise Him then the Merciful Lord exclaims at his ingratitude. He is astonished by this worst activity of his. He amazes over his ingratitude. He says:

"Say: " Who is it that delivereth you from the dark recesses of land and sea, when ye call upon Him in humility and in secret: if He only delivers us from these (dangers), (we vow) we shall truly show our gratitude? Say: It is Allah that delivereth you from these and all (other) distresses: and yet ye worship false gods" [1]

In the chapter of "Al Isra", He says:

"When distress seizes you at sea, those that ye call upon-besides Himself-leave you in the lurch! But when He brings you back safe to land, ye turned away (from Him). Most ungrateful is man" [2]

He continues saying:

" Yet when We bestow Our favours on man, he turns away and becomes remote on his side (instead of coming to Us), and when evil seizes him he gives himself up to despair" [3]

He further says:

" Do they not then see that We have made a Sanctuary secure, and that men are being snatched away from all around them? Then, do they believe in that which is vain, and reject the grace of Allah" [4]

Then ungratefulness is an unnatural thing. A wise man cannot like that. It is the activity of those who do not have brain in their skulls, light in their eyes, thought in their minds, understanding in their hearts and hearing power in their ears.

---

1) 6:63-64
2) 17:67
3) 17:83
4) 29:67

SATAN INVITES TO INFIDELITY

Here arises a question: Which thing does make them far from thanks and lead them to ingratitude and denial of God. In answer to this question, the Almighty Allah says:

" And on them did Satan prove true his idea, and they followed him, but a party that believed"[1]

"Zann" (Idea) is meant to determination of Satan before God upon misguidance of people, making them far from thanking God, the Creator of all universes and provoking them on ingratitude. He has challenged before God that he will do his best to misguide the people and to mislead them. He has said:

" I will mislead them, and I will create in them false desires; I will order them to slit the ears of cattle, and to deface the (fair) nature created by Allah" [2]

In the chapter of 'Al-A'raf' he is quoted as having said:

" He said: " Besause thou hast thrown me (out of the way), lo! I will lie in wait for them on the straight way: then I will assault from before them and behind them, from their right and their left: nor wilt Thou find, in most of them, gratitude (for Thy mercies).[3]

Then those persons who deny and condemn these countless proofs and don't thank God they are followers of Satan and these are the persons who fulfill his determination by their ingratitude and avoiding thank to God. In another word the worship of God is a kind of proof that the Devil is declared failed and that the man abides by the order of that who is powerful not only in this world but also in the Hereafter because Satan can work in this world only. As for the Hereafter, he will deny all things and will not stand to help his followers.

---

1) 34:20
2) 4:119
3) 7:16-17

MEANS OF THANKS

The Almighty Allah created man as His best creature. He gave him ears to hear, eyes to see and heart to think. After that he inspired him with good and bad qualities. Now the duty left for him is to utilize these abilities and to know God through these and then to thank Him and worship Him in a way He wants.

That's why these things are regarded as the best thing of the world and Heaven as the Prophet (SAWS) said:

" He who was given these four things is given the best things of the world and Hereafter; Grateful heart, remembering tongue, patient body on the calamity and a wife that does not want to cheat her husband about her and his money'[1]

He points to this fact:

' Say: " It is He Who has created you, and made for you the faculties of hearing, seeing, and understanding: Little thank it ye give" [2]

It is a fact that cannot be denied and even the infidels accept it on the Day of Judgment. They will say:

" They will further say: " Had we but listened or used our intelligence, we should not (now) be among the companions of the blazing fire" [3]

That's because the Prophet (SAWS) sought protection of God from an unbeneficial knowledge and fearless heart. He said:

" O Allah! I seek your protection from a knowledge that

does not benefit, a heart that does not fear, a soul that is not satisfied and a call that is not responded"[4]

Then the means of thanks are ears, eyes and hearts and the things which come out from these are: Hearing, seeing, knowing, wisdom, thinking, remembering, inclining to God, believing and desiring belief. All these qualities are mentioned in the Holy Qur'an. I quote some of these:

"Say: See ye if Allah were to make the night perpetual over you to the Day of Judgment, what god is there other than Allah, who can give you light? Will ye not then hearken?" And among His signs is the sleep that ye take by night and by day, and the quest that ye (Make for livelihood) out of His bounty: verily in that are signs for those who hearken" [5]

" Say: See ye? If Allah were to make the day perpetual over you to the Day of Judgment, what god is there other than Allah, who can give you night in which ye can rest. Will ye not then see? [6]

" And do they not see that we do drive rain to parched soil (bare of herbage), and produce therewith crops, providing food for their cattle and themselves? Have they not the vision" [7]

" If thou ask them, who it is that created the heavens and the earth. They will certainly say, "Allah", say: "Praise be to Allah" but most of them know not" [8]

" Say: Verily my Lord enlarges and restricts the provision to whom He pleases, but most men know not" [9]

" And from the fruit of the date-palms and the vine, yet get out strong drink, and wholesome food: behold, in this also is a sign for those who are wise"

" It is He Who gives life and death, to Him (is due) the alternation of night and day: will ye not then understand" [11]

" Then to eat of all the produce (of the earth), and follow the ways of thy Lord made smooth: there issues from within their bodies a drink of varying colours, wherein is healing for men: verily in this is a sign for those who give thought"[12]

" And among His signs is this, that He created for you mates from among yourselves, that ye may dwell in tranquility with them, and he has put love and mercy between your (hearts): verily in that are signs for those who reflect" [13]

"See they not what is before them and behind them, of the sky and the earth? If We wished, We could cause the earth to swallow them up, or cause a piece of the sky to fall upon them. Verily in that is a sign for every devotee that turns to Allah (in repentance).[14]

" And the earth We have spread it out, and set thereon mountains standing firm, and produced therein every kind of beautiful growth (in pairs for an insight and reminder to every servant, turning to Allah)"[15]

" And in creation of yourselves and the fact that animals are scattered through the earth, are signs for those of assured faith" [16]

"On the earth are signs for those of assured faith"?[17]

" And We sent down the Book to thee so that that thou shouldst make clear to them those things in which they differ, and that it should be a guide and a mercy to those who believe" [18]

" Know they not that Allah charges the provision or restricts it, for any He pleases? Verily, in this are signs for those who believe" [19]

These are things, which are related directly to God

who is invisible from our eyes but there is an indirect way to find this fact and that is to give thanks to the people who are moving among us and every time we face them from any way. That's why the Prophet (SAWS) said that the humanbeings are a source to extend thanks to God. If some one does not thank them he is not hoped to be thankful to God:

" Abu Horairah (RATA) narrates that the Prophet (SAWS) said: He who does not thank people does not give thank to God" [20]

That's why, in a tradition, their denial is regarded as "Kufr" (Paganism):

" Jabir s/o Abdullah (RA) narrates that the Prophet (SAWS) said; Let he who is presented with any gift, should also reward the giver the same and if he has nothing then he has to praise him so the person who praises him, thanks him but the person who hides it, denies it" [21]

---

1) MZ, 4:502
2) 67::23
3) 67:10
4) M, 6906
5) 28:71
6) 28:72
7) 32:27
8) 31 :25
(9) 29:62
10) 16:67
11) 23:80
12) 16:69
13) 30:21
14) 34:9
15) 50:78
16) 45:4
17) 51:20
18) 16:64
19) 39:52
20) T,1954
21) AD, 4813

Result of Shukr

When the sentiment for thanks-giving arises in a person's heart he naturally inclines to his Creator and a belief in the Oneness of God comes to fore followed by the belief in the prophethood. I deduce this idea from the order of the verses of the chapter of AlFatiha':

"Praise be to Allah the Cherisher and Sustainer of the worlds: Most Gracious, Most Merciful; Master of the Day of Judgment. Thee do we worship, and Thine aid we seek. Show us the straight way"[1]

So "Praise" leads a person to the worship of God, "Thee do we worship and Thine aid we seek" which is followed by the prophethood " Show us the straight way"

It is also clear from the coming verse of 'Al-Nisa':

" What can Allah gain by your punishment? If ye are grateful and ye believe? Nay it is Allah that recogniseth (All good), and knoweth all things"[2]

Then the sentence "If ye are grateful and ye believe" points out clearly that belief is a result of thanks-giving.

Now a person who is full of belief in God and the Prophet tightens his belt to pay his duty of worship to his Creator so that he would be real thanks-giver. The Holy Qur'an says:

" Nay, but worship Allah, and be of those who give thanks" [3]

And the best and the most perfect way of worship is Salah (prayer). So this thank leads a grateful person to Salah. The Almighty says:

" And remembers the name of his Guardian--Lord, prays" [4]

The boundary of thanks does not end here but it oversteps and comprises of all good deeds in all parts of human life. So obedience of parents, order of good, prohibition of bad, moderation in walk, aversion of voice, freedom of slave [5] ------- even belief in the life of the Herafter come under the results of thank. It is clear from the order of thanks-giving verses:

“We bestowed (in the past) wisdom on Luqman:" Show (thy) gratitude to Allah" Any who is (so) grateful does so to the profit of his own soul: but if any is ungrateful, verily Allah is free of all wants, worthy of all praise. Behold, Luqman said to his son admonishing him " O my son! Join not in worship (others) with Allah: for false worship is indeed the highest wrongdoing" And We have enjoined on man (to be good) to his parents: In travail upon travail did his mother bear him. And in years twain was his weaning: (hear the command), " Show gratitude to Me and to thy parents: to Me is (thy final) goal. “But if they strive to make thee join in worship with Me things of which thou hast no knowledge, obey them not; yet bear them company in this life with justice (and consideration), and follow the way of those who turn to Me: in the end the return of you all is to Me, and I will tell you all that ye did. " O my son! "(Said Luqman), if there be (but) the weight of a mustard-seed and if were (hidden) in a rock, or (any where) in the heavens or on the earth, Allah will bring it forth: for Allah is subtle and aware. " O my son! Establish regular prayer, rejoin what is just, and forbid what is wrong: and bear with patient consistency whater beside thee; for this is firmness of (purpose) in (the conduct of) affairs. "And swell not thy cheek (for pride) at men. Nor walk in insolence through the earth: for Allah loveth not any arrogant boaster. "And be moderate in thy pace, and lower thy voice; for the harshest of sounds without doubt is the braying of the ass"[6]

So monotheism, which is oneness of God in both the positive and negative ways, obedience of parents, their good and full service especially when they have reached the old age and are in bad need of any loyal and obedient servant. Mother is mentioned especially because she bears a lot in the process of upbringing a child. But do not accept their opinion that leads you to paganism, to joining anyother false god to Allah. It means that the right of Allah is the first and then the rights of the parents come. It also shows that if there were anyone to be worshipped on the earth then their were the parents only on the basis of their unselfish services to the child. The verse also shows that their difference of religious opinion do not stop their servives.

They are to be served at any rah the last verses show that all good features and manners an born from a more sense of thanks-giving.

---

1) 1 :2-6
2) 4: 147
3) 39:66
4) 87:15
5) 90:13
6) 31:12-19

Shukr is life

Why is a man born? It is only for eating and. sleeping, for doing business and enjoyment, for marrying and celebrating honey-moon, for capturing power and rule.? This is a question which quided some people while misguided lot of them. Those who thaught upon this sincerely and want through it rightly they wore guided to the right path. Its right answer is recognition of God through the inner and enter worlds of the man. And those who do not pay much attention to it and took it wally and insincerely they were really misguided and involed in the matters whose result is their failure in the Hereafter. Its wrong answer is to pay much attention to the world avoiding its Creator. Such people prefer mateial life and avoid spiritual life which is the eternal.

Its answer is given by the Creator thus:

"I did not create Jinn and men but to worship Me".[1]

So the person that does not worship Him is as though he was not created or in other words, he is dead and the person who is worshipping Him is alive even after his death.

"Don't say them dead but they are alive and you are not feeling" [2]

It is explained in the following tradition:

"The Prophet (SAWS) said: The person that remembers his Lord and that who does not rernember

Him are like living and dead".[3]

In another tradition, the persons are replaced by the houses:

"The house in which Allah is remembered and that in which He is not remembered are like living and dead".[4]

---

1) 51 :56
2) 2:154
3) B,6407
4) M, 1823

ADVANTAGES OF THANKS

The Almighty Allah is All-Aware and All-Knowing. He sees and notes every activity of His servants. He is nearer to them than their jugular veins:

" It was We Who created man, and We know what suggestions his soul makes to him; for We are nearer to him than (His) jugular vein" [1]

When a servant remembers and calls Him He listens and responds to it sooner or later. The Prophet (SAWS) said:

" Allah says: I am at the imagination of My servant of Me and I am with him when he calls Me: If he calls Me in himself I call him in Myself and if he calls Me in a group I call him in a group that is better than that. If he nears Me as far a span of the hand I near him as much as of an arm, if he becomes near to Me as much as of an arm I become near to him as much as of a hand and if he comes to Me on feet I come to him running" [2]

Then the person who remembers Allah and gives thanks to Him is rewarded a lot even if someone tries to count that he cannot do it. The prophet Sulaiman has said:

" Said one who had knowledge of the Book: "I will bring

it to thee before ever thy glance returns to thee. Then when (Solomon) saw it placed firmly before him, he said: "This is by the grace of my Lord!-to test me whether I am grateful or ungrateful! And if any is grateful, truly his gratitude is (again) for his own soul; but if any is ungrateful, truly my Lord is free of all needs, supreme in honour"[3]

The Almighty Allah says:

" We bestowed (in the past) wisdom on Luqman: "Show (thy) gratitude to Allah ."Any who is (so) grateful does so to the profit of his own soul: but if any is ungrateful, verily Allah is free of all wants, worthy of all praise"[4]

So the thanks-giver although does it for Allah but really he does it for himself because Allah gives more after that and increases what he has given him. These benefits are of two kinds:

1-One of these is related to the world.

2-The other is concerned with the heaven.

1-Advantages in the world: So in this life, He secures him from the worldly punishment, gives him good thing and increases what he has from his God. He says about the nation of Lut:

"The people of Lut rejected (his) warning We sent against them a violent tornado with showers of stones, (which destroyed them), except Lut's household: them We delivered by early dawn, - as a grace from Us: thus do We reward those who give thanks"[5]

After mentioning the thanks of Ibrahirn, He says:

" And We gave him good in the reward"[6]

He promises increase in the belongings only for thanks:

"And remember! Your Lord caused to be declared (publicly): " If ye are grateful, I will add more (favours) unto you; but if ye show ingratitude, truly My punishment is terrible indeed"[7]

2-Advantages in the Life after: As for the advantages in the Life-after, He makes the cause of the thanks-givers high and differentiates them from others. He says:

"Nor can a soul die except by Allah's leave, the term being fixed as by writing. If any do desire a reward in this life, We shall give it to him; and if any do desire a reward in the Hereafter, We shall give it to him. And swiftly shall We reward those that (serve us with) gratitude"[8]

So the sentence " Swiftly shall We those that thank" is not but only for honouring them and highlighting their importance.

Actually their advantages in the coming life are so much that you cannot count them. Their being innumerable is apparent from this verse:

" Now no person knows what delights of the eye

are kept hidden (in reserve) for them-as a reward for their (good) deeds"[9]

First of all He will pardon them and overlook their errors and sins[10]

" For men and women who engage much in Allah's remembrance for them has Allah prepared forgiveness and great reward"[11]

Then He will admit them in the group of pious people:

" And he will be, in the Hereafter, in the rank of the righteous"[12]

After that He will give them the same rewards given to these pious and fearing worshippers:

" As to the righteous, they shall drink of a cup mixed with Kafur,-a fountain where the devotees of Allah do drink, making it flown unstinted abundance"[13]

He elaborates these rewards in the above-mentioned chapter:

" But Allah will deliver them from the evil of the Day, and will shed over them brightness and a (blissful) joy. And because they were patíent and constant, He will reward them with a garden and (garments of) silk. Reclining in the (garden) on raised couches, they will see there neither the sun's (excessive heat) nor excessive cold. And the shades of the (garden) will come low over them, and the bunches (of fruit), there, will hang low easy to reach.And amongst them will be passed round vessels of silver and goblets of crystal,-crystal-clear, made of silver: they will determine the measure thereof (according to their wishes). And they will be given to drink there of a cup mixed with Zanjabil,a fountain there, called Salsabil. And round about them will (serve) youths of perpetual (freshness): if thou seest them, thou wouldst think them scattered pearls. And when thou lookest, it is there thou wilt see a bliss and a realm magnificent. Upon them will be green garments of fine silk and heavy brocade, and they will be adorned with bracelets of silver; and there Lord will give to them to drink a pure drink. Verily this is a reward for you, and your endeavour is accepted and recognized"[14]

In another place of the Holy Qur an we came across:

" Truly the righteous will be in bliss. On raised couches will they command a sight (of all things): Thou wilt recognize in their faces the beaming brightness of bliss. Their thirst will be slaked with pure vine sealed; The thereof will be Musk: and for this let those aspire, who have aspirations. With it will be (given a mixture of Tasnim:a spring, from) the waters) whereof drink those nearest to Allah"[15]

In short, they will be bestowed with all kinds of rewards and finally they will be permitted to enter the Heaven, which is the real source:

"And He has prepared for them a generous reward"[16]

"And remember Allah frequently that ye may prosper"[17]

I) 50:16
2) B, 2694
3) 27:40
4) 31:12
5) 54:33-35
6) 16:122
7) 14:7
8) 3:145
9) 32:17
10) The importance of the forgiveness of Allah is clear from the next tradition in which the Prophet (SAW) asked for it first: " O Allah! There is no life but of the Hereafter so pardon the Ansar (Helpers) and the Muhajirs (Migrants). B, 6414
11) 33:35
12) 16:122
13) 6:5-6
14) '16:11-22
15) 83:22-28
16) 33:44
I7) 62:20

SHUKR FREES FROM HYPOCRISY

A hypocrisy is a kind of show that you do not have. It helps in hiding what you have. So it is crystal clear that the thing, that you do not have and you show it only, will not remain forever. It will remain for a limited time to achieve some goals or to cheat some one and when you have succeeded in your intention would you come back to your previous or hidden condition. In spite of that, the person who is sincere in his aim and duty does not show it and will do it continuously. This continuity and regularity is a source that helps to know someone's sincerity and hypocrisy. The thanks-giving is one of these sources. Its continuity helps us to disclose someone's hypocrisy. To this point, the Prophet (SAWS) has pointed out saying:

" He who remembers Allah much is free from hypocrisy" [1]

That's why the meetings and circles of the remembrance are called as "the gardens of Jannah" because those who remember Allah sincerely have already been given permission to enter it. The Prophet (SAWS) said:

"When you pass by the gardens of Jannah, grass from it. They asked: What are the gardens of Jannah? He replied: They are the circles of the remembrances" [2]

In another tradition, it is very clear:

"The Messenger of Allah said: Some people remember Allah on the comfortable beds, Allah will make them enter the paradises".[3]

It is also known from this tradition that thanks-giving is wanted either it is in the palace or in the hut, in the airconditioned room or in the hot day. Reward of none will be less than the other. A rich and a poor are equal in paying this duty. But the trial of a rich is more dangerous than that who has no money.

---

1) JS, 2/579

2) T, 3510

3) MZ, 10/80

Consequence of infidelity

A person sometimes forgets the Almighty Allah and does not remember that he is the slave of a Creator who is merciful and powerful. He denies Him and does not thank Him. The Almighty Allah shows him how He has tamed the universe for him. For instance, he has a horse. How does he utilize it and how does he obey his orders. He serves him in a manner in which he desires. Such a person should think upon him and his horse. Such example has been given by that to take lesson from that:

"By the (Steeds) that run, with panting (breath), and strike sparks of fire, and push home the charge in the morning, and raise the dust In clouds the while, and penetrate forthwith into the midst (of the foe) enmasse, Truly Man is, to his Lord, ungrateful".[1]

In another place, He threatens of His power to destroy the whole earth and to throw a piece of His wrath from the sky:

"See they not what is before them and behind them, Of the sky and the earth? If We wished, We could cause the earth to swallow them up, or cause a piece of the sky to fall upon them. Verily in this is a Sign for every devotee that turns to Allah (in repentance)".[2]

But this man does not take care of that, forgets it and rolls out what was threatened. Then Allah sends a punishment from Him and from the earth. He destroys him and makes a lesson for others. It happened like that with the native people of Lut:

"The People of Lut rejected (His warning. We sent against them a violent tornado with showers of stones. (Which destroyed them), except Lut's household:: them We delivered by early dawn, as a Grace from Us: Thus do We reward those who give thanks".[3]

About the people of Saba, He says:

"But they turned away (from Allah), And we sent against them the flood (released) from the Dams, and We converted their two garden (rows) into "gardens" producing bitter fruits, and tamarisks, and some few (stunted) Lote-trees" [4]

He also says:

" We made them as a tale (that is told), and We dispersed them all in scattered fragments. Verily in this are signs for every (soul that is) patiently constant and grateful" [5]

There are a lot of instances for that in the Holy Qur'an. Everyone has to face the consequence of his deeds, good or bad.

---

1) 100:1-6
2) 34:9
3) 54:33-35
4) 34:16
5) 34:19

ABUNDANCE WITH INFIDELITY

Sometime a question arises in the minds of some believers: Why is an infidel increased in his money and children and why is a believer put to test.

To answer this question, we say that a believer is not suffering from poverty due to the punishment of God but He thus puts him to test to ascertain his belief and determination. And every believer whether the prophet or a common man, has to undergo that and to pass this test. There are ample examples of such in the lives of the prophets. See how the prophet Ibrahim was tested:

" And remember that Abraham was tried by his Lord with certain commands, which he fulfilled"[1]

The prophet Daud was also tested:

" And David gathered that We had tried him: he asked forgiveness of his Lord, fell down, bowing (in prostration), and turned (to Allah in repentance).[2]

The last prophet Muhammad (SAWS) was also put to tests:

" What ye suffered on the day the two armies met, was with the leave of Allah, in order that He might test the believers, -and the hypocrites also"[3]

He continues to say:

“Allah will not leave the believers in the state in which ye are now, until He separates what is evil from what is good" [4]

It is very clear in the chapter of "Al Taubah" :

" Do you think that you would be left alone while Allah has not yet known those among you who strive with might and main, and take non for friends and protectors except Allah, His Messenger, and the (community of) believers? And Allah is well-acquainted with (all) that ye do" [5]

So it has become a rule and tradition for every one who wants to be a true believer and to show his firmness:

" Thus did We test some of them by others, that they should say: "Is these then that Allah hath favoured from amongst us?" Doth not Allah know best those who are grateful"? [6]

As for the increase in the money and strength of an infidel, that is only a respite given to him:

"If Allah were to punish men according to what they deserve, he would not leave on the back of the (earth) a single living creature: but he gives them respite for a stated term: when their term expires, verily Allah has in His sight all his servants" [7]

In another place, He said:

" If it were Our will, We could drown them: then would there be no helper (to hear their cry) , nor could they be delivered, except by way of mercy from Us, and by way of (worldly) convenience (to serve them) for a time" [8]

He also said:

"As for them, they are but plotting a scheme, and I am planning a scheme. Therefore grant a delay to the unbelievers: give respite to them gently (for a while).[9]

The examples of bringing gradually are numberless. Here are some of them:

" Let not the unbelievers think that Our respite to them is good for themselves: We grant them respite that they may grow in their iniquity: but they will have a shameful punishment" [10]

"Then leave me alone with such as reject this Message : by degrees shall We draw them on little by little from directions they perceive not. A (long) respite will I grant them: truly powerful is my plan" [11]

" The Ad (people) rejected the Messengers. Behold, their brother Hud said to them: " Will ye not fear (Allah? " I am to you a messenger worthy of all trust. So fear Allah and obey me"---------" Do ye build a landmark on every high place to amuse yourselves? And do ye get for yourselves fine buildings in the hope of living therein (for ever) ----Ye ----Ye fear him Who has bestowed on you freely all that ye know. Freely has He bestowed on you cattle and sons, and gardens and springs. -They said: it is the same to us whether thou admonish us or be not among (our) admonishers. ------So they rejected him, and We destroyed them." [12]

In short, they are given these things only to delay their end. And a believer should not be cheated by his plotting.

---

1) 2:124
2) 38:24
3) 3:166-167
4) 3:1'19
5) 9:16
6) 6:53
7) 35:45
8) 36:43-44
9) 86:15-17
10) 3:176
11) 69:44-45
12) 26:123-139

Priority Of Thanks

Man is tested in two ways: abundance and lack. Some times, he is given abundance of wealth, children and power and some times all these things are taken away from him and he becomes empty-handed and helpless. The question is: Which of these is more dangerous?

It would become clear from the study of The Holy Qur'an and the traditions of the Prophet (SAWS) that the majority of those who oppressed and misled are rich and powerful persons. When they were given a test in the matter of wealth, health, power and progeny, they would not pass it:

" Your riches and your children may be but a trial: whereas Allah, with Him is the highest reward" [1]

" When some trouble toucheth man he crieth unto his Lord, turning to Him in repentance: but when He bestoweth a favour upon him as from Himself, (may doth forget what he cried and prayed for before and he doth set up rivals unto Allah, thus misleading others from Allah's path. Say: " Enjoy thy disbelief for a little while: verily thou art (one) of the companions of the fire" [2]

" When We give him a taste of some mercy from Us, after some adversity had touched him, he is sure to say," This is due to my (merit): I think not that the Hour (of judgment) will (ever) be established; but if I am brought back to my Lord, I have (much) good (stored) in His sight! But We will show the unbelievers the truth of all that they did, and we will give them the taste of a severe chastisement. When we bestowed favours on man, he turns away, and gets himself remote on his side (instead of coming to Us); and when evil seizes him, (he comes) full of prolonged prayer!" [3]

The Prophet (SAWS) said: I do not fear poverty of your but I fear that the world would be expanded for you as it was done with those who went before you then you compete one another as they did and it would divert them (from the remembrance of Allah) as did with those who were before you" [4]

There are a host of examples of those who forgot the real path only because they were given all facilities in their lives. Some of these are as follows:

" And the chiefs of his people, who disbelieved and denied the meeting in the Hereafter, and on whom we had bestowed the good things of this life, said: " He is no more than a man like yourselves: he eats and drinks of what ye drink" [5]

" Never did We send a Warner to a population, but the wealthy ones among them said: We believe not in the (message) with which ye have been sent." They said: We have more in wealth and in sons, and we cannot be chastised" [6]

It is accepted by those who will face God's punishment on the Day of Judgment:

" The Day He will gather them together as well -----as those whom they worship besides Allah, He will ask: "Was it ye who led these May servants astray, or did they stray from the path themselves? They will say: Glory to thee! Not meet was it for us that we should take for protectors others besides Thee: But Thou didst bestow, on them and their fathers, good things (in life), until they forgot the Message: for they were a people destroyed".

Here is a story of two persons, which is told in the Holy Qur'an. It is the best example for that:

" Set forth to them the parable of two men: for one of them We provided two gardens of grape-vines and surrounded them with date palms; in between the two We placed the tillage. Each of those gardens brought forth its produce, and failed not in the least therein: in the midst of them We caused a river to flow. (Abundant) was the produce this man had: he said to his companion, in the course of a mutual argument:" More wealth have I than you, and more honour and power in (my following of) men. He went into his garden while he wronged himself: He said: " I deem not that this will ever perish. Nor do I deem that the Hour (of judgment) will (ever) come: Even if I am brought back to my Lord. I shall surely find (there) something better in exchange. His companion said to him, in the course of the argument with him: " Doest thou deny Him Who created thee out of dust, then out of a sperm-drop, then fashioned thee into a man? But as for my part Allah is my Lord, and non shall I associate with my lord. Why didst thou not, as thou wentest into thy garden, say; " Allah's will (be done)! There is no power but from Allah!" If thou dost see me less than thee in wealth and son, it may be that my Lord will give me something better than thy garden, and that he will send on thy garden thunderbolts (by way of reckoning) from heaven, making it (but O slippery sand!) Or the water of the garden will run off underground so that thou wilt never be able to find it. So his fnuts were encompassed (with ruin), and he remained twisting and turning his hands over what he had spent on his property, which had (now) tumbled to pieces to its very foundations, and he could only say, " Woe is me! Would I had never ascribed partners to my Lord and Cherisher! Nor had he numbers to help him against Allah, nor was he able to deliver himself. There, the (Only) protection comes from Allah, the True One. He is the Best to reward, and the Best to give success.[8]

That's why God has warned us from committing such dangerous things:

" O ye who believe! Let not your riches or your children divert you from the remembrance of Allah. If any act thus, surely they are the losers" [9]

---

l) 64:15
2) 39:8
3) 41:50-51
4) B, 6425
5) 23:33
6) 34:34-35
7) 25:17-18
8) 18:32-44
9) 63:9

SABR (PATIENCE) AS AN EXPRESSION OF SHUKR

A believer thanks his God in two states: In his happiness and in his sadness. Happiness is a result of some boon-related occurrences by the will of God. But sadness is a kind of test sought by God to show the world that that person whom He loves and prefers to others is not in vain but a great person and does all his activities according to the will of God. This is the cause behind his priority. So keeping patience is also a kind of Shukr though in differently.

That's why it is narrated from the Prophet that he said:

"The person who suffers from fever at the night then keeps patience and is satisfied by God, comes out of his sins so as he was at the time of birth"[1]

In another narration we come across as follows:

"Allah says: When I took some one's the dearest thing then he keeps patience and hopes reward, I will not agree for him with a reward less than Jannah"[2]

It is crystal clear from this tradition:

"The Prophet (SAWS) said: A believer is full of wonderful things. All his affairs are good. It's only for him; If he meets with a happiness gives thanks. It's a good for him and if he suffers from a calamity and keeps patience then it's also good for him"[3]

It is the reason behind this saying of the Prophet (SAWS):

" The great reward is accompanied with the great (severe) trial"[4]

---

1) TR, 4/299
2) T, 2401
3) M, 7500
4) RS, 33

When and where will you thank?

It's very clear that the Power that deserves to be thanked is God, the Cherisher of the worlds. But, as I mentioned in the chapter titled "Means of thanks" a man who helped you also deserves it. The Prophet (SAWS) said to a person who gave him debt:

"May Allah bless you in your family and money. The return of debt is not but to thank and to pay back, (Payment)".[1]

It's one side, but there is another side of it. All creatures including man are the servants of God. So the person, who gives thanks to them or meets them in their happiness and problem, visits Allah and serves Him and the person who does not do it does not serve Him. This is very clear from a tradition narrated by Abu Huraira:

"The Prophet (SAWS) said: Allah will ask on the Day of Resurrection: O man; I was ill but you did not visit Me. He will reply: O my Lord! How can I visit You. You are the Cherisher of the worlds. He will say: Did you not know that so and so servant of Mine was ill and you did not visit him. Did you not know that if you had visited him you would have found Me there. O man! I asked food from you but you did not feed Me. He will reply! O my Lord! How can I feed You. You are the Cherisher of the worlds. He will say: Did you not know that so and so servant of Mine asked food from you but you did not serve him. Did you not know that if you had fed him you would have found it with Me. O man I asked water from you but you did not give it to Me. He will reply: O my Lord: How can I give you water while you are the Cherisher of the worlds. He will say: So and so servant of Mine asked you water but you did not give him. Did you not know that if you gave him water you would have found it with Me".[2]

So the services of every creature is the service of God who had created him.

As for the time of thanks, it is not specified. You can do it when you want but you have to do it as much as you can. And every thing you take is from Him so you have to give it out at that moment. Here are some traditions that show it very clearly.

"The Messenger of Allah said: The first who will be called to Jannah are those who praise Allah in happiness and sadness".[3]

"The Messenger of Allah said: He who said at the time of getting up in the moming. The boon that I found in the morning is only from you. So you are praised and thanked, paid his thanks of the day and he who said it in the evening paid it in the night".[4]

"The Messenger of Allah said: The inhabitants of Jannah will not mourn anything except a time that passed by them and they did not give thanks to Allah"[5]

All the prayers and calls taught by the Prophet (SAWS) consist of thanks-giving.

---

1) N, 4687 2) M, 6556 3) Z, 1/502
4) AD, 5073 5) 1S, 2/468

Qualities Of Thanks-Givers

Before winding up this topic, I must mention the qualities and activities of those who pay thanks to their Lord. It will help those who want to be like them to select the better path and to work on that. Now, a thanks-giver, due to search for realities and facts, does not fall quickly upon any thing like a blind person but looks into the origin then searches for it and its Creator. So he finds what is known to others:

"Seest thou not that Allah makes the clouds move gently, then joins them together, then makes them into a heap?-then wilt thou see rain issues forth from their midst. And he sends down from the sky mountain masses (of clouds) wherein is hail: he strikes therewith whom He pleases and He turns it away from whom He pleases. The vivid flash of its lightning wellnigh blinds the sight. It is Allah Who alternates the night and the day: Verily in these things is an instructive example for those who have vision"[1]

He goes through the expanse of universe, intricacies of body and contours of the history:

" Seest thou not that the ships sail through the ocean by the grace of Allah? -that He may show you of His signs? Verily in this are signs for all who constantly preserve and give thanks"[2]

" Between them and the cities on which We had poured Our blessings, We had placed cities in prominent position, and between them We had appointed stages of journey in due proportion: Travel therein, secure, by night and day,"

But they said: "Our Lord! Place longer distances between our journey-stages". But they wronged themselves (therein). At length We made them as a tale (that is told), and We dispersed them all in scattered fragments. Verily in this are signs for every (soul that is) patiently constant and grateful" [3]

"If Allah were to enlarge the provision for His servants, they would indeed transgress beyond all bounds through the earth; but He sends (it) down in due measure as He pleases. For He is with His servants well-acquainted, Watchful. He is the one that sends down rain (even) after (men) have given up all hope, and scatters His mercy (far and wide). And He is the Protector, Worthy of all praise. And among His signs is the creation of the heavens and the earth, and the living creatures that He has scattered through them: and He has power to gather them together when He wills. Whatever misfortune happens to you, is because of the things your hands have wrought, and for many (a sin) He grants forgiveness. Nor can ye escape through the earth; nor have ye, besides Allah, any one to protect or to help. And among His signs are the ships, smooth-running through the ocean, as mountains. If it be His will, He can still the wind: then would they become motionless on the back of the (ocean). Verily in this are signs for every one who patiently preserves and is grateful"[4]

" We sent Moses with our signs (and the command)." Bring out thy people from the depths of darkness into light, and remind them of the days of Allah." Verily in this there are signs for such as are firmly patient and constant, rateful and appreciative" [5]

The person who thinks sincerely must be fearful of Lord and believer in these evidences:

" Only those believe in Our signs, who, when they are recited to them fall down in adoration, and celeberate the praises of their Lord, nor are thy (ever) puffed up with pride." [6]

" They forsake their beds of sleep, the while they call on their Lord, in fear and hope: and they spend (in charity) out of the sustenance which we have bestowed on them"[7]

" And so amongst men and beast and cattle, are they of various colors. Those truly fear Allah, amongst His servants who have knowledge; for Allah is exalted in might, Oft-forgiving" [8]

And that who fears from Allah believing in the signs of God, must be a good worshipper and spends his life according to His orders:

" And the servants of (Allah) Most Gracious are those who walk on the earth in humility, and when the ignorant address them, they say, "Peace!"; Those who spend the night in adoration of their Lord prostrate and standing; those who say," Our Lord! Avert from us the wrath of Hell, for its wrath is indeed an affliction grievous, evil indeed is it as an abode, and as a place to rest in", those who, when they spend, are not extravagant and not niggardly, but hold a just (balance) between those (extremes); those who invoke not, with Allah, any other god, nor slay such life as Allah has made sacred, except for just cause, nor commit fornication;-and any that does this (not only) meets punishment (but) the chastisement on the Day of Judgment will be doubled to him, and he will dwell therein in ignomity,- unless he repents, believes, and works righteous deeds, for Allah will change the evil of such persons into good, and Allah is Oft-forgiving, Most merciful, and whoever repents and does good has truly turned to Allah in repentance: those who witness no falsehood and, if they pass by futility, they pass by it with honourable (avoidance); those who, when they are admonished with the signs of their Lord, droop not down at them as if they were deaf or blind; and those who pray, " Our Lord! Grant unto us wives and offsprings who will be the comfort of our eyes, and give us (the grace) to lead the righteous" [9]

He elaborates some other qualities:

"They perform (their) vows, and they fear a day whose evil flies far and wide. And they feed, for the love of Allah, the indigent, the orphan and the captive, (saying), " We feed you for the sake of Allah alone: no reward do we desire from you, nor thanks. We only fear a day of frowning and distress from the side of our Lord"[10]

Then the thanks-givers are those who will say on the Day of Judgment after looking at rewards given to them in the Jannah:

" (This will be) their prayer therein: "Glory to Thee, 0 Allah!" and "peace" will be their greeting therein and the end of their prayer will be: "Praise be to Allah, the Cherisher and sustainer of the worlds!" [11]

They will also say:

" They will say:" Praise be to Allah, Who has truly fulfilled His promise to us, and has given us (this) land in heritage: we can dwell in the garden as we will: how excellent a reward for those who work (righteousness)![12]

---

l) 24:43-44	2) 31 :31	3) 34:18-19
4) 42:27-33	5) 14:5	6) 32:15
7) 32:16	8) 35:28	9) 25:63-74
10) 76:7-10	11) 10:10	12) 39:74